W9-BWT-197

Essential Jobs

We Need Food Workers

by Brienna Rossiter

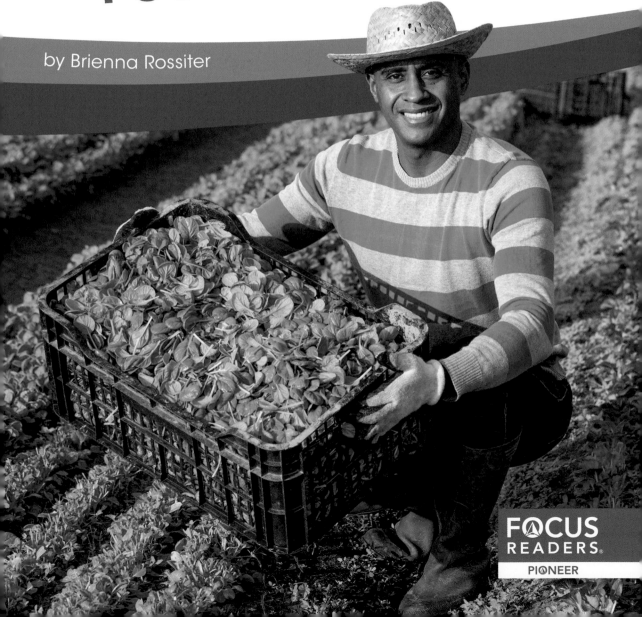

FOCUS READERS

PIONEER

www.focusreaders.com

Focus Readers is distributed by North Star Editions:
sales@northstareditions.com | 888-417-0195

Produced for Focus Readers by Red Line Editorial.

Photographs ©: Shutterstock Images, cover, 1, 4, 7, 8, 11, 12, 15 (top), 15 (bottom), 17, 18, 21

Library of Congress Cataloging-in-Publication Data
Library of Congress Cataloging-in-Publication Data is available on the Library of Congress website.

ISBN
978-1-63739-031-3 (hardcover)
978-1-63739-085-6 (paperback)
978-1-63739-192-1 (ebook pdf)
978-1-63739-139-6 (hosted ebook)

Printed in the United States of America
Mankato, MN
012022

About the Author

Brienna Rossiter is a writer and editor who lives in Minnesota.

Table of Contents

Chapter 1

The Food Supply

People eat food every day. Food comes from many sources. Fruits, grains, and nuts come from plants. So do vegetables. Meat, eggs, and cheese come from animals.

Getting food to people involves many steps. First, workers grow the food. Next, they **harvest** the food. Then, they get the food ready to sell. They send it to people and stores.

Fun Fact

Some foods grow only in certain places. So, people **ship** the foods around the world.

Chapter 2

Food Production

Many people work on farms. Some workers help raise animals. Workers feed and care for animals. They help the animals stay healthy.

Other workers plant and harvest **crops**. For some foods, people use tractors or other machines. Other foods are picked by hand. Groups of workers gather them.

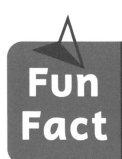

Fun Fact

Many fruits are picked by hand.

Chapter 3

Getting Food Ready

Many workers help get food ready to eat. Some work at factories. They help **process** and package food. They also do tests to make sure the food is safe.

Other workers send food to restaurants and stores. They plan where it needs to go. Then they load it on trucks or other **vehicles**. They make sure the food is stored safely, too.

Fun Fact

Many foods must be kept cold. Otherwise, they will go bad.

Food Factories

Factory workers make or clean many foods. Machines mix **ingredients** together. Then the machines heat or cool the food. They put the food in packages, too. People **operate** these machines. They make sure the machines work correctly. Workers may also sort or count food.

Chapter 4

Selling Food

Many workers cook and serve food. Some work at restaurants. Others bake food that is sold in shops or grocery stores.

Workers also help people buy food. Some workers fill the shelves at stores. They try to make sure supplies don't run out. Other workers help **customers** pay for food.

Fun Fact

Some people deliver food for stores or restaurants. They bring orders right to people's homes.

FOCUS ON
Food Workers

Write your answers on a separate piece of paper.

1. Write a sentence describing one job that workers might do on a farm.

2. What is your favorite food to eat? Why?

3. Which job might a worker at a food factory do?
    - A. plant crops
    - B. sort food
    - C. sell food to customers

4. Why would stores want to make sure they don't run out of food?
    - A. If stores run out of food, they will need more workers.
    - B. If stores run out of food, they will make more money.
    - C. If stores run out of food, customers can't buy it.

Answer key on page 24.

Glossary

crops
Plants that people grow to eat or sell.

customers
People who buy things from a store or restaurant.

harvest
To collect something so it can be used as food.

ingredients
Foods that are mixed together to make a meal.

operate
To use or control a machine.

process
To change a food by adding something to it or by preparing it in a certain way. This may include freezing, canning, baking, or drying the food.

ship
To send something to a different place.

vehicles
Machines that carry things from place to place. Boats, trucks, trains, and airplanes are some examples.

To Learn More

BOOKS

Murray, Julie. *Grocery Store Workers*. Minneapolis: Abdo Publishing, 2021.

Raij, Emily. *Farmers*. North Mankato, MN: Capstone Publishing, 2021.

NOTE TO EDUCATORS

Visit **www.focusreaders.com** to find lesson plans, activities, links, and other resources related to this title.

Index

Answer Key: **1.** Answers will vary; **2.** Answers will vary; **3.** B; **4.** C